Life Ain't A Dress Rehearsal

Lives in Poetry

by

Cecil D. Haas

Life Ain't a Dress Rehearsal
© 2023 Cecil D. Haas
All Rights Reserved

Published by
Indy Pub

Cover Photo by Cecil D. Haas

Cover and text design by Faye Henry

No part of this book may be reproduced or transmitted in any form or by any means, electronic or mechanical, including photocopying, recording, or by any digital or information storage and retrieval system, without permission in writing from the author.

First Edition
Printed 2023

ISBN 9781088106501

Library of Congress Control Number: 2023910578

This book is dedicated to the friends who have
given me so much support.

They will find themselves in these pages,
because this is a collection of their experiences,
as well as mine.

Table of Contents

Title 1
Publishing Information 2
Dedication 3
Table of Contents 4
Introduction 9
Poems
    Life Ain't a Dress Rehearsal Poem 10
    A Love Story 11
        Beginning 12
        Hot Tub Heaven 12
        The Wordsmith 13
        The Edge 14
        The Wind Has Changed 15
        Libby's Sonnet 15
        Growing 16
        Give Me Your Hurts 17
        When Leaves Fall 17
        Across the Miles 18
        Crossroads 18
        Trained 19
        Freedom's Captive 19
        Thank You For Another Day 20
        Understanding 20
        Something 21
        Seeds 21
        Coming Back 22
        Fear of Change 22
        Beyond Reach 23
        Love's Sleep 23
        Chance 24
        Love To Share 25
        Thoughts Shared 25
        Sanction 26
        Today 26
        Separation 27
        By Choice 27
        Time For Love 28
        Thanks 28
        The Gift 29
        I Saved Your Place 29
        Flip Side of Love 29
        Routes And Reasons 30
        Who We Are 30
        Consequences 31
        Awakening 32
        Together 32
        First Meeting 33
        Overrun 33
        Existence 34
        Bet You Can't Love Just One 35
        Marriage 35
        Alive 36

December Spring 36
The Reflection 37
Names 37
Our Time 38
Falling Stars 40
Falling Stars 2 40
Rainbows 41
Intimacy 41
I'm Just A Man 42
Measurement 43
I Hesitate 43
Happy Ever After 44
Fear 45
Loss And Gain 45
The Desert 46
Chapter Two 47
Logic 48
Illusion 48

Loss 49

Investment 50
Package Deal 50
Alone 51
Relief 51
How Long 52
Exile 52
Spring Camp Fire 53
Theft 53
Apparition 54
Real And Ideal 54
Harvest 54
Decisions 55
Going Home 55
The Catch 56
The Lesson 56
Stood Up 57
Time Is Unkind 57
The Man I Used To Be 58
The Way You Are 59
Ownership 60
Past Illusion 60
Rape 61
No Regret In The Dry Ravine 61
Ropes 62
The Passing 62
Limits 62
When Dreams Die 63
I Remember You 63
Rules 63
The Birthday Cake 64
Rebellion 64
Cannibals 65
Leaving 66

Ramblings 67
- Signs 68
- Tribute To Man's Thoughts 68
- Don't Spit Agin' The Wind 69
- Second Start 70
- The Idol 70
- All's Fair 71
- Ode To Orange 71
- Beyond Compare 72
- Impedance 73
- May 73
- On Co-Existence 73
- Home Came To Me 74
- Last Card 75
- Bad Times 75
- Chicago Airport 75
- Time Is Life 76
- Whatever Owns You 77
- Trilemma 77
- Abuse 78
- Heaven And Hell 78
- Decisions 80
- Repentance 80
- End of The Season 81

Vietnam 82
- Wars Priority 83
- The Journey 83
- Vietnam Calls 84
- Long Distance 84
- The Green Fields of January 85
- I Got My Nail 85
- Paper Hero 86
- Looking Back 87
- Our Debt 88

People 89
- Pop's Last Visit 90
- Our Time 90
- Tribute To My Son 92
- Free Man 93
- The Girl In Line 94
- Freedom 94
- Judy And Me 95
- Allways 95
- Ken 96
- Dreams 96
- Fuel 97
- Pilots 97
- Indoor Plumbing 98
- Laine 99
- Tessa 99
- Retreat 100
- The Barrier 100

- The Homeplace Fire 101
- My Mark 101
- The Pace 102
- April 102
- The Guide 103
- Help 103
- Old Photographs 104
- The Battle 105
- No Thanks 105
- Passion 106
- Chance Meeting 107
- Flight 107
- The Ones That Got Away 108
- Everybody Dies 109

Outdoors 110
- Worlds 111
- Time Laughs 111
- The Feather 112
- Just One Last Cast 116
- The Hunt 117
- Our Cabin In The Hills 119
- My Place 120
- Alaska Summer 121
- Man VS Nature 122

Mending The Break 123
- First Steps 124
- Out Of Touch 124
- Time Is Kind 125
- April 30th 125
- The Firemakers 126
- Fulfilled 126
- My Love Grows Near 127
- The Wish 128
- For All The Wrong Reasons 129

My Daughter 130
- Jennifer At Eight 131
- Jennifer At Twelve 132
- Jennifer At Sixteen 133
- Jennifer At Twenty 134
- Jennifer At Twenty-Four 135

Love Waits 136
- The Wait 137
- Back From The Brink 138
- Behind The Need 138
- For Love And Duty's Sake 139

Furry Friends 140
- Daisy And Me 141
- Boomer 142
- Grey Cat 143
- A Death In The Family 144

About The Author 145
Acknowledgements 146

Life Ain't A Dress Rehearsal

Lives in Poetry

INTRODUCTION

If I wrote for gold

I'd be hungry and cold

I write for my friends' and my

Protection from

The desperation

I see in old men's eyes.

My name on a bank

Would be a terrible prank

When me and my friends are gone

But I live without age

If on one page

One line lives on and on.

Life Ain't A Dress Rehearsal

What if life was a dress rehearsal
With always a second scene?
Would we live it with more abandon
Or stay with the same routine?
How would we prepare for the final act
And what would we optimize?
Would we carefully tend the balance sheet
Or joyously live our first lives?

Would we learn more from first doing everything right
Or doing a lot of things wrong?
Would we carefully save the best for last
Or laugh at our chances blown?

We can look at our lives and know the answer
For all of our best and worst,
We would play both acts the very same way
Both tragedies, last and first.

Yet this I have learned from my only time through
With few tomorrows to lend,
We can't prepare for happiness
By saving it all til the end.

CDH 11/06

A LOVE STORY

Love is not love that alters when it alteration finds.
　　　　　- William Shakespeare

　　Once upon a time (and once upon a place also),

　　There was you, and there was me.

　　And there and then, against the odds,

　　 You and me became us ………

BEGINNING

It's truly love and not obsession
For we are free, not just possessions
Free to live, and free to be;
I'll lean on you, and you on me.
Let past hurts go, we both will win;
Let life and love begin again.

HOT TUB HEAVEN

The sun has set, and evening's chill
Promises yet another thrill;
We drop our towels as we go in
Leaving our modesty behind.

Like skinny-dipping in the creek –
The funest kind of hide-and-seek –
We tiptoe in and touch and giggle,
From wine's release and bubble's tickle.

But now I share this with the one
Who fate has made my one true love;
Who adds depth to child-like play
As we talk and share our day.

What a wondrous place to be,
Immersed in pleasure, you and me,
Feeling all our aches and troubles
Dissolved with wine and love and bubbles.

THE WORDSMITH

He was a craftsman
The words obeyed his will.
He had learned that words
Were power
To hold, control, manipulate.
He learned that no idea
However good
Could happen without words;
That no intent
However low
Could be checked
If proper words were found;
That rhetoric and logic
Could be interchanged.
Each aspect of the art and craft
Were studied, practiced, studied, practiced
And he was seen as wise
And viewed as deep
When words were chosen well.
And words became the man.
Then a word was given
Which defied the forge;
A word which, in itself
Held other words;
A word which changed and redefined
The purpose of all words
And that word became the man.
Words still are penned and spoken
But now as cascades from a mountain stream
Without intent but to express
The master word.
Not to manipulate or hide
But to reveal
The man, the word.
The forge has been rekindled
With a gentler fire
Since you gave me the word
And all it means.

THE EDGE

Let's teach each other the thrill of the edge
To commit and gamble it all
Pick the direction and not look down
To fly we must risk the fall.

Enslaved by the things we dared not do
Now driven by those we must
If we break away those tired, old bonds
We'll have nothing to cling to but trust.

Trust that we are forever
Trust that our lives will mend
Trust that love will indeed win out
Trust of the thrust toward that end.

THE WIND HAS CHANGED

The wind has changed
The time has come to sail.
I've things to do
That must be left undone.
I've friends on shore
That I may never see again.
There's more unknown than known
Yet if I am to cross
It's time. The wind has changed.

LIBBY'S SONNET

Determined, tenacious and focused
To achieve nothing less than the goal;
Discounting, ignoring detractors
Commit, press on body and soul.
Yet loving, encouraging partner
Who picks me up when I fall
Who lifts me when life is the bleakest
Who trusts and accepts through it all.
And you nurture, excite and thrill me
As you hold me in your arms.
For all that we are, I love you.
With you there's no fear of the storm:
My haven, my refuge from strife;
My friend, my lover, my wife.

GROWING

As I matured
I learned how not to dream
Or trust instincts
However real they seem.
I grew instead to trust
What could be proved
And lived a sadness borne
Of absolutes.
And now – eighteen again
And learning how to feel
Love, with just a touch
Of what is real.

GIVE ME YOUR HURTS

We're friends.
Your smiles and dreams
I'll gladly share.
But not just these;
Give me your hurts,
I'll handle them with care.

WHEN LEAVES FALL

When leaves last fell
They spoke of loss and death.
It was a time to morn what was
But mostly what was not.

When leaves last fell
I was adrift and lost
Wondering what was to be
And where was my place.

Again it's time;
Fall's chilly nights
Have turned the green to gold
And when I see my breath
It tells me I'm alive.

You came to me
After leaves last fell
And made this a season when
You, like the leaves,
Fill my life with color.

ACROSS THE MILES

My love reaches out across the miles
Remembering good times, remembering smiles.
Knowing you're mine will warm me tonight;
Knowing I'm yours makes the stars more bright.
My lady, my lover, my life;
My world, my woman, my wife.

CROSSROADS

Fear to go on -
      Anxious steps in unfamiliar darkness.

Fear to not go on –
      Escape the once complacent sanctuary.

Fear of the changing here and now
          That can't stand still.

Fear to touch
        Or be beyond your reach.

TRAINED

Please understand
I have been trained
To thrive on being almost close,
To stay just long enough
To recognize and key upon
The need to disinvolve
Then not to cling.

The armor which
Then served me well
I shed with you.
To feel the softness of the grass
On my bare skin
Means I must risk
The pain of thorns.
In faith, not fear
I now stand resolute with you.
I am – and will be – here
But please understand
I have been trained.

FREEDOM'S CAPTIVE

I'm yours. I'm bound
A willing captive of your love
Yet I now feel more free
To think, to feel, to be.
Love is a door that I've walked through
But into freedom, not confinement
Into the warmth where I belong
And with no door knob on this side
There is no chance of going back
To be indentured to the past.

THANK YOU FOR ANOTHER DAY

Every morning when I wake up I think of you.
I remember those wonderful things about you;
How beautiful you are, inside and out;
How loving and giving you are;
How exciting you are;
How much fun you are.
And again I fall in love with you,
Even more deeply than the day before.
Thank you for loving me back.

UNDERSTANDING

I stand in awe

Of things I feel for you

Without a threat;

Of things I say

That come without the calculations;

The things I do

That work out right;

The things I think

That you think, too;

But most of all

That you understand.

SOMETHING

I like things the way they are.
Perhaps they should be different.... better
Maybe we struggle for perfection
And in doing so
Kill something of beauty
For what it can never be.

SEEDS

We planted seeds

Then waited through

The long cold winter.

When the time was right --

Seeds somehow know --

They emerged through new-warmed earth

To greet the sun

That wasn't there just yesterday.

COMING BACK

A letter born of loneliness
A song conceived in sorrow
Your last touch only moments old
I shiver to think of tomorrow.
I'll smile at the usual meeting
And they, smiling back, cannot know
My smile is for another
I touched but hours ago.
Another who waits and wonders;
Another who also smiles
Through pangs of the lonely hours
My love across the miles.

FEAR OF CHANGE

I remember
Wanting you so much
Before I went away.
Years ago.
This time
Things were different
We loved all night
Curled toes
Peeled paint off the ceiling
Until I had to catch the plane.
Yet I felt the sting
Like years ago.
I'm coming back
But scared
It just felt too much
Like good-bye.

BEYOND REACH

Did I dream you?
Are you a grand illusion
Of happiness I can never really have;
The warm spring wind through winter's forest;
The drifting, flowing, changing tide
That controls my every unseen mood?
A day not somehow shared with you
Is as a night without stars,
Sleep without dreams.

LOVE'S SLEEP

How sweet the sleep lovemaking brings

Crossed by shadows of unremembered dreams;

The lull that comes between the joys

Of sharing your night and your morning.

CHANCE

Is it wise for me to care too much
And could I if I tried?
Can I again tear down the walls
Or will I come just close enough
To mitigate the risks
And not expose
Those parts of me so easily hurt?

Can I again become a part
Of something that can crush my hopes
Is there reason to believe
What I so crave can be achieved
Only knowing love that hasn't worked?

Can we go on
When what we have is safe
Do we dare reach for more?
How many things of beauty
Might we kill?

Can we carefully engage
That we may gracefully retreat
Or must we leap
Into a dark unknown?
Can love take a calculated course
And go where it must go?

And what is fair to you?
I cannot know your needs
For love and trust
Nor ask you to incur the risks
To a life that keeps you safe;
A haven from love's past heartaches.

The risks were so much easier to take
When I knew all the answers
It's not today I fear
But the change tomorrow brings.

LOVE TO SHARE

Love is a moment

    A time

        A place.

But people change

    And places change

        And time goes on

Don't promise love undying

    For you may stay

        For promises alone

Tomorrow will come

    I've love to share today.

THOUGHTS SHARED

Perhaps I think - or dream - too much
Or lack the courage to rather do.
But I have never hurt a person
With a thought.
You may share my day - or life,
But you must know in knowing me
That only I must justify
My thoughts, and then to only me.
With you I'm free
To think aloud.
I'll stop
When I have to answer why.

SANCTION

That which we feel and do some question
Unsanctioned by the laws of man or deity,
But those lesser bonds have sooner fallen
To those they'll never see.
Not within man's law
For those who do not understand compare;
But there's a place within His plan
For this rarity we share.
Should I yet decades chance to see
If not enchanted still,
Then I stand here condemned,
For doubters hear: I did, I do, I always will.
When my heart so resounds,
I cannot bid it stay within my stale true bounds.

TODAY

Today I woke again
Without you by my side.
Today time moves so slowly
As I watch the clock and count the hours.
Today I busy myself
With chores already done.
Today you're coming back;
Anticipation changes now to joy
Today I no longer have to feel
Your love across the miles.
Today
My world again becomes complete.

To Renee, with love.

SEPARATION

I cannot speak of the sadness
That replaced my time with you
They cannot know of unsanctioned pain
I'll bear your absence through.
A part of my world is missing
I seek comfort that equals your touch
No person to know and share my day
Is the price for caring too much
You're gone for a time or forever
The fire now warm may grow cold
Who knows of the changes that time will bring
Or our divergent paths may mold.

BY CHOICE

I am the third
To ever touch you.
Quite an honor.
There's the first
That everyone has
And a husband.
Some have dozens
But not everyone
Has a third.

TIME FOR LOVE

Love lives, and touches me each day
No matter how bad the day
No matter how long the day
For time for love
Takes no time from my day.

THANKS

Then you.
And life was new.
I felt, I breathed, I knew
What life meant - you.
If I would choose or will
I still could not forget.
When my last heartbeat stills,
If as in quiet sunset
Or on disputed hills,
These thoughts live yet:
Of those remembered times
Your love was mine
That happy time
Our lives entwined.

THE GIFT

There was a poem in me
I wrote for you
And gave to you
Because it was yours.

I don't remember what I wrote
Those years ago
Though I will not forget
The love that made me write.

I SAVED YOUR PLACE

Welcome back.
I knew you'd come
Across the miles
I saved a place for you.
I knew you were the one
And so was I.

FLIP SIDE OF LOVE

A golden ring, a tender kiss,
And words, endless words.
A moonlit night
And want,
Music: slow, soft, enticing,
Comfort, never ending
Picnics, parties, people –
By all means never be alone.
Money, Yes, a must
For who is anyone without?
And trust? Essential.
Within eyesight of course.
A trip? The beach? Why not?
For after all there'll always be
This never ending present.
Grasp! Take! Own! Consume!
For this is love and can't exist
Without all this

ROUTES AND REASONS

So many nice things happened
For all the wrong reasons.
I've met real people
On paths they chose -
Right or wrong.
Maybe I took the wrong turn
At some now forgotten intersection
But somewhere in my journey
Two nice things made worthwhile
Each futile mile:
I found myself
And I found you.
What would I change?
Only some injustice
I have done
But not my path
Who knows
I might have overlooked
Some things most dear.

WHO ARE WE

I know you

I know me

But who are we?

CONSEQUENCES

Deep feelings cause deep chasms
If I seem to overreact
To small things that you say and do
It's because I see and hear
Too much unsaid by any phrase
Too much inferred by any gesture.
It's me, not you.
Please understand
I think I try too hard
Perhaps I'm too fine tuned
To you.

AWAKENING

Love is its own reward or curse
A reaching for that which cannot be
Without its own destruction
So I've heard.
And I believed
For lack of evidence
That something else was true
And out of old remembered hurts
Which overshadowed
All the smiles.

But as with all rules
It crumbled with exception
Now I must dare to care
Or find another wall to hide behind.

For love is still alive and well
How strange this was to know
Until you touched my fingertips
And reached my soul.

TOGETHER

I cherish the time you share with me;
Your warmth that seems never to cease;
The closeness that brings my heart joy;
Your sweetness that fills me with peace.

FIRST MEETING

I'm looking back on our brief chat
That's now just hours old
Its memory and what the future has to hold.

Did you hear what I meant
And not just what I said?
Was it as it should be
Or did it show
The lack of confidence - or fear-
I felt that you would just say no.

But you said yes...YES!
And then I wondered if you saw
The pleased surprise I felt.
Was I able to conceal
My eagerness to see you sooner, longer
Or could you tell?

So now with midnight mellowed memory
I smile -
Part at myself, part at the day just past
And hope you're smiling, too.

OVERRUN

I tried to go slow
I tried not to show
That I let things get so out of hand.
It's a pleasure to know you
But heaven to love you
Even if loving you wasn't part of my plan.
You've awakened my feelings
Long forgotten but true
You're just too hard to know
Without loving you.

EXISTENCE

For one accustomed
To some continuous present
Tomorrow is a concept
Hard to live for.
Now days are spent
Uninvolved, aloof
In waiting for
Some time yet to be
Hoping that I won't again
Become immune.

BET YOU CAN'T LOVE JUST ONE

You've cheated and lied
I've believed you and tried
To think that you might someday change.
You say you love me
But I plainly see
That heartache's the name of your game.
There's something inside you
That makes you feel tied to
Some ways that I can't understand.
You've hurt me so long
That I can't play along
And I can't be a part of your plans.
When you're through having fun
When there's no place to run
When all's said and done
Bet you can't love just one.

MARRIAGE

I want you for my very own
But could we survive the strife
That seems to come to everyone
When they become husband and wife?
I love your wild free spirit
And thrill at your tender touch
Could you wake up beside me each morning
And still not be stifled too much?
I know why you stay -- you care
There are no ties but your love and mine
But I know you revere the contract
And the promise that's said for all time.
Some sad day we may stop loving
I hope that day never comes
I just want the times to get better
And never be with you while being alone.

ALIVE

Midnight, and Monday morning
Stole you back.
And I went home alone
And savored all night long
The thoughts we shared.
And dreams were dreams again
Not just what might have been.
I dared to feel
Those feelings so long gone
With high school optimism
Tempered with the wisdom
I didn't have back then.
Last night
I lived again.

DECEMBER SPRING

December came and was almost gone
Her cold, short days
All life – like mine
Asleep.
Spring was so far away.

Then you came in my life
And filled my life with you,
Your warmth,
Your Springtime love,
And my world with sunshine days.

THE REFLECTION

Who is this person that I see
In mirrors looking back at me
Whose smiling face is all aglow
So different than short months ago?

When love came unexpectedly
And changed my course to calmer seas
She gave my life a brand new start
She came to me and took my heart.

We both were worn by heartbreaks past
With futures loveless, overtasked
When things were looking bleak and black,
I saved her; she saved me back.

With love so sweet I hardly know
The me of three short months ago.

NAMES

Whether it be good or evil,
Hate, or lust, or love,
Why do we not correctly name
What we are fearful of?

Ignore it and it can't ensnare
We're free to plod along
Within the bounds of comfort
In lives that we've built walls around.

The norms where we are hurt-proof
Worlds we can exist within
Rooms safe and lonely we can lock
And let nobody in.

When will we venture outside walls
That shielded us so long
And face what we're MOST fearful of
When will we call it love?

OUR TIME

I have been a part
Of many lives;
Some for a fleeting moment,
Some still remain.

And they are a part of mine;
I saw the world
Throught many eyes,
So it was always new.

I am now composed
Of all the paths and passions
Of all the hopes and dreams and loves
Of those held dear.

Our paths would merge
And often then diverge
Some with a smile
And some with tears.

I hope we truly shared.
But I can only judge
What I received;
I hope I gave as much.

I tried to show to each
Their special gifts.
I made them – for the most part – smile;
I hope that they still do.
I truly tried
To make our time a special time,
To – for a while –
Completely be a part of us.

I tried to glean
The best and special parts of love,
To not sink in the tedium
Of promises unkept.

(continued)

(Our Time Continued)

But the thing I could not give
Was any promise of tomorrow,
Assurance that things would not change,
Or would.

Perhaps these other lives and loves
Have kept me now from being close,
Prevented ties exclusive and unique,
Assured a future loneliness.

Each ended, yes,
But our time did not starve for love
Or long for soon-lost dreams
Or die the normal lengthy, painful death.

FALLING STARS

Look up!
There are falling stars to wish upon.
And, if you choose,
Me there
To help those wishes come true.

FALLING STARS 2

I cannot schedule
Falling stars
For cloudless nights;
But they are there,
Sometimes obscured,
But there.
I cannot clear away the clouds
Of old, past hurts.
But wait
Clear nights will come
When we can wish,
And together,
Make a wish come true.

RAINBOWS

As tears of old hurts dry,
As clouds of doubt part and drift away,
The sun breaking through the lingering mist
Will form a lovely double rainbow for us,
A promise of a brighter path ahead.

No storms of doubt or hurt
Will come between us or our love.
Any rain that comes to us
Now we'll weather hand in hand,
And smile at our rainbows when the sun shines through.

INTIMACY

I know more of you
Than everyone together.
Seen in your eyes
Those looks for me alone.
You have let me look
Into the depths of you.
I can at once
Bask smugly in unquestioned love
And tremble at your trust.

I'M JUST A MAN

When you look at me
Through love-filled eyes
I know I'm not
As good nor wise
As you perceive.

But know, my love,
And understand
Amid your love
I'm just a man
Just hoping to achieve.

I'll do my best
Each day for us
I'll sometimes fail
I hope you'll trust
It's not to peeve.

So when you find
My imperfections
I hope you don't
In deep reflection
Regret you didn't leave.

MEASUREMENT

I do not need
A measure of your love.
I will never ask
How much you love me.

I see it in your eyes;
I feel it in your touch;
I hear it in your voice;
I know it in my heart.
You give your love to me
So freely without bounds
To ask "How much?"
Would ask, "How deep your soul?"

To measure love you give
Or measure love I give to you
Would be as big a task
As to measure life itself.

I HESITATE

Sometimes I hesitate to tell you:

How much I love you
Because I am afraid
You will see me as desperate.

How much I want you
Because I'm afraid
You will see me as shallow.

How much I need you
Because I'm afraid
You will see me as weak.

HAPPY EVER AFTER

They lived happy ever after
So ends the fairy tale
The triumphs and the trials passed
The story's plot would stale.

So there's nothing left to write
All glory has been told
Just breathe and breed and pass each day
Til bodies are stiff and cold.
Love pales and then is redefined
So it's hard to separate
From comfort and complacency
Is this its destined fate?

Until you I could accept
That happy ever after means
Stagnation of the impetus
To strive, to grow, to dream.

Just when I thought the saga through
The real tale has yet to be told
For loving you has clearly shown
Love is the only worthy goal.

A goal that's never quite achieved
Or prove those old assumptions true
A climax where love's sweetness peaks
I cannot ever love you through.

FEAR

Fear of change
Exceeded by the fear of where I am.

Fear of never loving - Or being loved
That overshadows fear of love.

Fear of passion overwhelmed
By fear of passion lost.

Fear of heights
That draws me to the edge.

LOSS AND GAIN

Sometimes I think
I'm leaving everything.
Then I remember love;
How things were
Before you.

Then I realize
I'm leaving nothing
For everything of value –
For us
For all I've dreamed of.

THE DESERT

One hour we have been apart
And yet I long for you
As if it had been weeks.
How less than whole I feel
How I anticipate and focus on
The next time I will feel you close.
So much that time alone
I spend as plodding through
Some barren place.
The destination only matters
A goal that keeps me traveling toward
The next brief time we'll share
The next oasis where we'll quench our thirst
Then on again
Until we find our place and time.

CHAPTER TWO

The plot must change
The conflicts rise
And loves are weighed.

An epic grand
Left to unfold
Just started now
And yet we're bound.

We must live
Each day in turn
And word by word
Our story told.

That story interlaced
With others' lives
A web which moves
With each strand touched.

The hurts and joys
Must have their time
The characters revealed
The climax reached.

So many pages
Left to turn
Before the happy
Ever after end.

LOGIC

Events have started to unfold
And step by step we disinvolve
We weigh each action and each word
And focus just on our resolve.

Yet I am so confused and weak
I seem to so much need the time
To gather strength from being near
And rest from scripts and lines.

Still logic says to lower risk
Just smile and play the game
You've now tasted truth and love
But you must behave the same.

Logic says you must deny
Don't let your feelings show;
The feelings that you thrive upon
Are fuel for the goal.

Logic says "Be patient!"
The hours go so slow
And logic asks how much I care
But logic cannot know.

ILLUSION

Could this be real
Or the joy of one night shared
A memory steeped
In weeks of thoughts of you?

We touched –
Our fingertips, our lips, ourselves
I had to go
I was afraid, and promises to keep.

But seeds long dormant
Growing now
In the warmth
Of coming near again.

LOSS...

Relationships end. There are unintended consequences.
For many reasons, people who were once part of our lives are gone.
We change. These things are a part of life,
and they shape our lives.....

INVESTMENT

I sat alone last night
Wanting time with you
Knowing that it could not be
For some time yet to come.

Sacrifice seems needed now
Investments made today
To pay tomorrow's dividends
To live then well.

Time alone and darkness plot
Against the daytime optimism
Nurtured by the moments here and there
I shared with you.

They whisper of the risks
Too great to be incurred
But not the necessary gains
Of being us.

Where does investment stop
And speculation start
That ended with the broken bodies
Underneath the windows
In 1929?

PACKAGE DEAL

I slipped between the sheets

Still fragrant from our love

Delight matched only

By the sadness

Of being here alone.

ALONE

I've done a dozen things today
To chase reality away
I've done quite well
Most folks can't tell
How utterly alone I feel.

But now the day is finally done
And I'm by choice all alone
The world appears as shades of gray
The soft pastels of yesterday
All left with you.

I wonder what tomorrow brings
And shiver as I rearrange
Priorities to match the need
Disregarding feelings freed
That I must now deny

The stars are just not quite as bright
As I sit alone tonight
Not as distinct, not quite so near
Perhaps the wine, perhaps the tears
Our heaven misses you.

RELIEF

My friend darkness
I have missed you.
Now the days grow longer
More time must be spent
Behind a mask
Involved with trivial distractions
Until appropriate time
That I can claim fatigue
Go to my room
Turn off the light
Cry out the pent up tears.

HOW LONG

I cannot touch you now
You belong to him again
Only with my eyes
Am I allowed to touch your skin.
Only with my memories
Am I allowed to savor you.
Our every moment spoken for
There is no time for us.
To love someone you don't
Seems too harsh a punishment
While mine is to wait
Who knows how long?
Perhaps forever.

EXILE

I am alone – alone
A thousand miles alone.
Have I always been alone?
Will I forever be alone?
Did I belong?
Anywhere to anyone belong?
To something larger than myself belong?
Or just to loneliness belong?
I hurt.
The laughter dies, I hurt.
No one to see, I hurt.
No one to be, I hurt.
Outside, alone, I hurt.

SPRING CAMP FIRE

Charred blackened ruins.
High green haven lost.
Cold ashes still scorch my soul
What waste – what cost.

Gone – only in my mind
I'll track your ridges till darkness falls
Drink from your springs, smell your spruce
Seek shelter by your canyon walls.

Now man made you as man
Used, abused, and short of life
Devoid now, yet in your finest hour
You lived to rise above his strife.

THEFT

I waited by the phone
Two hours past the time
You said you'd call.
I would have understood
If you had just said no
I've heard those words before.
That truth is a finger prick
Drawing just a bit of blood
And soon forgotten.
Resentment soon replaced anticipation
And bled all humor from my day
Changing smiles to questions why.
There is no more cruel way
To steal my day
Than say
Your time is of no value.

APPARITION

A knock
And standing at my door
A lovely apparition
That stayed just long enough
To untie the strings
Which I so neatly tied.
Too real to be a dream
Too elusive to be real
And gone so soon.
What makes me wait
For hours by a phone
I don't expect to ring.

REAL AND IDEAL

Driven by our discontent
When our ideals don't match our roles,
This void steers us to
Unsought direction and unreasoned goals.
Ignoring or obscuring truth
Of heart or hardship cost
We venture for imagined gain
So soon, so lost.

HARVEST

Does our toil go unrewarded
Is there no harvest after all?
With branches bare from winter
Our cupboard seems empty and small.
We're reminded by past summer's memory
By dried rose petals on the ground
The rose is for only a season
The thorns will last year round.

DECISIONS

How trivial decisions are
That count for us alone,
But how complex the slightest thing
That touches lives beyond our own.

We move as one and complement
We live in worlds quite far, yet near
Being together makes other ways
Seem unimportant and unclear.

How easy it would be tonight
To promise you forever
Forget the past and alter worlds
For things we dare not savor.

GOING HOME

Home to love
Home to changes met by changes
Home to those who look
For something different than what I am.
To expectations, fears
And intentions that never quite get done.
Home to only leave again
And wonder if it's worth the hurt
That caring brings.

THE CATCH

Involvement --
I thrived on it
Til you came
I played the game
Very well
I usually won.
Now I sit
Alone
In an empty room
Afraid.

THE LESSON

I closed my eyes, my ears, my heart
To truth, to logic, fact.
I saw just what I liked to see,
Rose colored glasses saw to that.
Love sees itself, a fool's mirage,
And seeks its own for need,
For fallacies so plainly there
It will not, can not, heed.
Though I unwisely dared to care
And knew it couldn't last
I'm wiser now for having loved you
For one reckless moment past.

STOOD UP

Two hours late
And working on forever.
I only wish I didn't care;
I wish that you didn't matter.
Listening for the telephone
That doesn't ring
Gets so much harder every time
I've grown to despise the thing.
It eats at my mind
And tears at my thoughts
I dare not go, nor stay
Chained to the expectations
That grew throughout the day.
The anticipation I felt all day
Makes a torture of being alone,
And makes me listen for a knock
I know won't come.

TIME IS UNKIND

Time sometimes is unkind
It says I cannot give
All the joys you need.

But I can today
Give you a kind of love
You've never had.

This candle still will glow
When you must go
When I must let you go.

THE MAN I USED TO BE

I wonder why your love chose me
Even the man I used to be.
And I'm not now as young or fair
Since the grey has touched my hair.

I was not even then that grand,
Far from being your ideal man.
I fell short in so many ways
Even in our earlier days.

Even before the surgeon's knife
Had taken vital parts of life
Taking the little that remained
Leaving just desire retained.

Some thrills of youth forever gone
Perhaps I deserve to be alone;
My life spared for added years
Is paid for with the nights of tears.

You still have so much to give
Is this the way you want to live?
I wonder why you still love me;
I'll never even be the man I used to be.

THE WAY YOU ARE

My memory has been kind to you
I still see you often as I wish --
And sometimes more -- in my mind.
You're still smiling
The sad smile which said
I'm sorry you're going
But glad you're coming back
And neither of us knew
It was good-bye.
We still walk in the park
And beside the river
We still make plans
We still love -- everywhere.
Your mom still cooks for me
Your dad still doesn't trust me ...
Perhaps he shouldn't after all.
You're still beautiful
Hair the color of wheat
And eyes as blue
As western skies.
It's always somewhere in between
The twentieth of March
And September twenty-second
And you're still seventeen.
I'm a different person now
From miles and years
And wear and tear
But time's been kind
To give me everything
But you.
I'm glad you're still the same
For if your memory changed
I feel that I might lose the right
To think of you as mine
To love you
The way you'll always be.

OWNERSHIP

I wandered through the fragrant woods
To contemplate the day just past
And by my unmarked path there stood
A single flower clinging to a fragile mast.
I wondered how it came to be
Unlike all else that grew around
I stooped that I could closer see
What, but by chance, would be unfound.
It seemed to bloom for love alone
Blushed to greet me as I kneeled
And with emotion still unknown
I reached and picked and killed.

PAST ILLUSION

You made it plain
The role I play
Or rather, don't.
The part
I guess
That bothers me
Is not where I stand
But where I stood.

RAPE

I saw someone who
Reminded me of you
I hurt clear through
Ashamed.
Remembering the time
You loved
I fed a line.
A cruel game
Rape by any other name.

NO REGRET IN THE DRY RAVINE

The water from the swiftly running stream
From honeysuckle shrouded hills
Though it gives life its very roots
Will stagnate when it stills.

My life's course must parallel
The dictates of dynamic time
Lest love stand still and quickly die
In compromise of staying what I am.

The here and now and circumstance
Demands of weakest links their test
For disaccord can either build or break
So I must stay, or go a friend at best.

Then let it here be love renewed
Or let it be an end
And throw no flowers on the grave
Of things that might have been.

ROPES

Whether to secure, or bind, or hang
For your consolation or despair
All ropes degenerate
From age, neglect, or wear and tear.

THE PASSING

When you came drifting through my world
I would have never guessed
That you'd be so soon gone
And you'd be so long missed.

Hours were only moments
Words blurred with too many drinks
But your face is etched in my mind
You're a part of each thought I think.

You're gone, I suppose forever
I'll accept it because I must
But you were just so soon gone
And you'll be so long, long missed.

LIMITS

You are my greatest need
Yet unfulfilled;
One need which saps all satisfaction
Of other triumphs;
Elusive happiness which dangles
Just beyond my reach
Though I throw myself
Against unyielding bars.

WHEN DREAMS DIE

Where do dreams go
When they die
Whether killed or starved?
They leave so big a hole
For emptiness and grief
But fill that space
They will.

I REMEMBER YOU

It's been a year
Since I last saw you
Since I last touched you.
We could have made it work ...
At least a while
We almost loved.

RULES

We knew what the rules were
When we played a game
So close to love.
Like children who climb trees
To flirt with gravity.
If I could change the rules
I'd live all my life today.
But I'm just one small part
Of something I can't stop
That now moves on.
Sadly I'll go
Helpless to do otherwise
That was also in the rules.
We had moments
And in those moments
Almost loved.

THE BIRTHDAY CAKE

It felt so good
To bake your cake.
There wasn't time to cut it.
You had to hurry.
I said I understood.
So I cut a slice
To save for your return
Then you came, and left again.
Tonight I unwrapped the slice.
Why was the chocolate bitter?
Tomorrow's garbage day.

REBELLION

The course I chose with pride
To shape my life before we met
And then forsook for only emptiness,
I've made believe, in vain, I could forget.

I find I cannot compromise
To make you happy, dear,
So my only and my last request
I beg of you to hear.

And if you find you can't accept
These things that I foresee,
Or if you find I can't fit in,
Then set me free:
The strict demands your way of life entails –
Don't try to shape my will to meet,
Unless you want to find your broken hopes and plans
Some morning at your feet.

CANNIBALS

I am a need
Because I satisfy a need
My being but what I provide.
For each need satisfied
More subtle needs arise
The unrelenting urgency the same.
I am strong
Because I must be strong
Even when I tremble.
Even as I grope in darkness
I must chart the course;
I must lead.
I am less a person
When expectations overlap
And I must choose.
I am to most
A set of expectations to be met;
What I can provide.
The farmer reaches deeper in the sack
Hogs must be fed.
The empty sack discarded
Of no use.
Arise and play the roles
I am the need.
Love is the need fulfilled.

LEAVING

I looked back as I started to the plane
You said you could not come
I said I understood
But I still looked back.

I changed my watch
It shows we're just an hour apart
Why does it seem
So far?

RAMBLINGS....

Each day things touch our lives as we go about the business of living.

Some are pleasant surprises, some are a distraction,

some change the course of our lives.

SIGNS

No dogs

No parking

No bicycles

Keep right

Keep moving

Keep off the grass

I don't know

What scares me most

Signs

Or fools that make them necessary.

TRIBUTE TO MAN'S THOUGHTS

Given pen and ink and time
Alone and free to think
And forced to sit and ponder
Or put his thoughts in ink,
Does he write of money and power
Or shrines in marble and paint?
Does he write of chances of fortunes
Lost by some turn of fate?
He neither writes of high ideals
Nor status nor social mores
He writes of life and love and lust
On the backs of bathroom doors.

DON'T SPIT AGIN' THE WIND

When I asked my father
At the tender age of ten
For a motto for success, he said,
"Don't spit agin' the wind."
I laughed and went my merry way
And took for jest this tool;
To spit against the wind, I thought
Would surely take a fool.
Well halfway through my schooling
They said I needed to go far
I was looking on to better things
So I quit school and bought a car.
As smart as I was sure I was
More education was a sin.
When I told pop he just said,
"You spit agin' the wind."
But I was happy for a while
With my hot rod and a buck
Cause all it takes to get ahead
Is just a little luck.
When I started looking up again
It didn't seem quite fair
For a genius like me
Not to be a millionaire
This set me back a peg or two
Cause it was quite a slam
But a man who'd surely know my worth
Would be my Uncle Sam.
I knew some things that he should know
Then found I hadn't known them first,
And when it came to changing him
I should have tried the universe.
I pulled the hitch without the luck
I counted on to make me shine,
But when it came to progress
I wasn't even marking time.
So again I plagued my father
For a formula to win.

"Just like I told you once" he said
Don't spit agin' the wind!
"The road that seems so rough and slow
Is just exactly that, with shortcuts few.
It's honest, it's the common road
The best of men all know it's true.
"Stand up for things you know you should
And fold those losing hands,
Don't fight the things that you can't change
Or let things go you can.
Success might wait at any turn
Just like a rainbow's end
So work, and think, have faith,
And son,
Don't spit agin' the wind!

SECOND START

With years since I last wrote
I begin, afraid,
Time has dulled
The edge that I once honed.
Pausing, halting, slowly
Words form in my mind.
I wonder if I can again
Pull whole coherent thoughts
I've feared to think
From deep within.
The forge must be rekindled
And values weighed
And risks incurred
As I'm forced to look
At two-dimensioned truth,
At all I am.
Verse cannot deceive
It mirrors clear
The soul.

THE IDOL

John Wayne can't die
There's outlaws to be dealt with.
The stunt men
Might let the Indians win.
There'll be nobody left
To hold our mirror.
We could follow him through blizzards
And never feel the cold;
Through hell
And never singe our boots.
John Wayne can't die
What will Glen Campbell do?

ALL'S FAIR

In this old world of make or break,
Of failure or of fame
It's scored by if you win or lose,
Not how you play the game.
You can sleep on dreams of being right
And dine on maybe's smiles,
But once you say, " I'm number one "
It beats all that a mile.
I've won a few and lost a few
And when all is said and done,
It's great to say you played it straight,
But heaven if you won.

ODE TO ORANGE

Take blue...
There's hue and new and you;

And apple....
For lack of anything else, there's dapple.

Or red...
Has said.

Even pear...
It just isn't fair,

For the poet whose favorite is orange,
Both the fruit and the color, a curse;

No matter how smart or how hard he tries,
It just can't be put at the end of a verse.

BEYOND COMPARE

Life was fun and simple
With no more than basic needs
A fishing pole, a swimming hole
My bath was in the creek.
With biscuits in the kitchen
And a soft straw tick at night
Tomorrow never mattered
Being poor was not a plight.
    For Spring was in the air
And I was rich beyond compare.

Spring gave way to Summer
And love's complicated tastes
I left the farm for bigger worlds
Houses, cars, and far-off places.
The world spread out before me
My course was mine to choose
I drank the sweetest wine of life –
How did this pass so soon?
    But Summertime was there
And I was rich beyond compare.

The things that matter still remain
The loving friends still stay
But the green's turned gold and crimson
The brown is flecked with grey.
The Grandkids crowd around me
There's stories to be read
And hugs and kisses all around
As I tuck them into bed.
    Autumn time is here
And I'm rich beyond compare.

I know the Winter's coming
When the days grow short and cold
Let me grow warm and loving
As I grow ever old.
Let me bask in love and life well spent
And always mellow stay
Not deal in things that might have been
So I can smile and say
    When winter time is here
That I'm rich beyond compare.

IMPEDANCE

In our time-spending world
A verse was wrought,
A noble mental hair,
Elusive, half-real thought.
Why did you not bless someone else
So duty could implore
The forging from a traveled pen;
Could these learned, madded masses dare ignore?
Were you here but several decades past
What scathing satire could you mold
From some poet's molten mind
But here you plague a pauper's mind grown cold.

MAY

Here's to you, arch-instigator,
You one and thirty meter funeral march
Prelude to the death in June
That dooms the male to collar starch.
Bring your half-revealing promises,
Damp April has accented by the waiting.
Man's only hope is indecision,
So many's there for mating.
With life at a complacent lull
Bewitched by honeysuckle,
All nature beckons come, partake,
But enslavement isn't natural.
Would anything like May in green
Make cares and common sense unseen?

ON CO-EXISTENCE

The pen may prove, where thoughts are free
Mightier than the saber be;
The script may rule a people literate,
Whereas, the blade be indiscriminate.
Let's trade our swords for brotherhood,
Only when sure the others would.

HOME CAME TO ME

It did?

Where? One home? Two homes?

What makes it so?

What makes it no more so?

Yes, love remains

And always will.

But somewhere in my journey

Home came to me.

LAST CARD

It's time to bet.
With one card left to take,
Do I gamble all I have
On make or break?
Heights of elation? Depths of despair?
The price of a card will tell,
A chance at one is a chance at both,
To dare to live is to know it well.
But you know something important,
It hurts, but it's not the end
When you draw a club to a diamond flush
You lose and you play again.
Because of the chips on the table,
The risks that seem so great
Make victory's savor sweeter -
Or more bearable defeat.

BAD TIMES

While just the feeblest falter during life's ideal
With courses on a smoothly charted main,
Be not dismayed by trying circumstance,
For lives, like rope, are proven only under strain.

CHICAGO AIRPORT

Chicago airport.
Assault to eyes and ears.
I like wood.
Like Albuquerque.
But I like trees
So glass and steel will do
In Chicago.

TIME IS LIFE

Time, the utmost gift of life,
Imprisons man to by-the-hour wage
To waste the sun and rain and waterfall
When measured by some round, unseeing face.

Behind a desk
Or thirty stories up on steel
So insecure that we buy
Half our day, plus weekends.

We watch the clock
That tells of time, but not of life
To serve some god called social order
And regulates our regimented strife.

There are songs to sing and hills to climb
And life and love that should be felt
Time was given, not to meter
Or compromise our very self.

WHATEVER OWNS YOU

Assault to all of value
And yet the show must go on
To be all opportunity offers
To be true to the pattern alone.
We are happy, ah yes, we're successful
In spite of our ransomed soul
For after all, the freedom we've lost
We'll repurchase ten times at our goal.
I'm not a rebel, I follow its lead
I waste sunsets and waterfalls
My time is my life, and my time is bought
To love or to loath it all.
Success is a simple matter;
Wealth, but a mountain to scale
But when I am old, can I looking back
Say to myself, "All is well."

TRILEMMA

I wish that I could live three lives,
Each one devoted to a cause
Each one distinct and quite apart
Free to choose without the other's loss.

In one I'd be the loving father
Who soothes and mends each family hurt
Who lives to guide and to protect
Whose destiny puts others first.

The second man is the achiever
Who has the plan to climb all hills
Who has the strength to conquer in
The worldly contest of strong wills.

But the one which I keep hid away
Is one who'd drink from nature's spring,
Who would exchange it all for time
To write, to be, to love, to sing.

ABUSE

Solicitors in airports
Protected by the first amendment
Whose draftsman
Never had to catch a plane.

HEAVEN AND HELL

Some say it is our lot to dwell
Eventually in heaven or hell
No in betweens or shades of grey;
Their god will choose: they receive or pay.
Their same god made the world to be
Not evil or good, but in between.

Nevertheless on judgment day
We'll form a line with our deeds displayed.
Those who stand at the head of the line
Get to go right in to a heaven sublime,
While those who are standing near the end
Will be cast into hell for their terrible sins.

But what of us, the common mass
Who will stand in the middle waiting to pass
Through the pearly gates in heaven to dwell
Or thrown to the horrible fate of hell?
We stand and wonder if we passed
Even if we weren't at the head of the class
Will He curve the grade, will I make a C
Or enough for a happy eternity?

Then some arbitrary henchman of God
Walks down the line with nary a nod,
And at a place where he sees fit
Will hold out his arm and say, "This is it!"
Those who stand at the henchman's right
Are permitted to go to the city of light.

(continued)

But the best of the worst and those behind
May as well have been at the end of the line
With those like Hitler and Idi Amin
And other slime as evil and mean.
The worst of the best will never feel
The lapping of hell's fire at his heels
Though there is little to separate
His deeds from the last one through hell's gate.

I think I know too little to tell
Whether there is a heaven or hell.
Just what it takes to pass through the gate
I know too little to speculate.
But if eternity doesn't exist
I believe it matters not one bit.

Live life as you know you should;
In spite of tomorrow, the good are the good.
Not for a reward for following rules
Or like the carrot in front of the mule.
If the world is a mess and you don't care
You're missing the point of being here.
If you live your life for eternity's sake
You'll never make it through the gate.

And what can be said of the concept of hell?
I believe it a horrible, fictitious tale
Born in some zealot's devious mind
To inflict his dogma on his own kind.
Whether it's real, or hot, or cold
Hell is a hell of a crowd control!
If you have such fear of the heat intense
To act to avoid the consequence
From fear – pure fear – you play along
You've been duped, and your motives are wrong.

And what of God, who devised the Plan
And shaped the universe with His hands?
I figure my mind is much too small
To understand one who understands all.
But I believe, and am content,
That truth works together and all makes sense.

DECISIONS

The wrong decision often guides our way
More true than if, by chance,
We picked a way less painful.
There are so many things
I could have done
That counting all the ifs that brought me here
I find myself a product more
Of those things I chose not to do
Than these I chose.

REPENTANCE

Here I sit my head a-throbbing
And the TV way down low
Half amused and idly wondering
Why I drink and party so.

Is it boredom, is it sorrow,
Is it just I can't say no?
I should change but know I won't
Because I love the night life so.

But this ain't a time for thinking
Of directions or of goals
On this laid back hung over Sunday
Looking at the Super Bowl.

END OF THE SEASON

I cut the grass today
The last time for the year.
The catcher picked up colored leaves.
But for the chill,
The lawn still thinks it's spring

The hardy marigolds
Still lend a color patch.
I let them stay.
They'll brave the frost
Another time or two.

I picked the last tomato.
The freeze tonight
Will get the rest.
They set too late this season
To show me a blushing cheek

But what a glorious year!
The spring and summertime
And even early autumn's joys
The long, hot days
The almost too-warm, moist nights.
I savored all the fruits;
Strawberries in the spring,
The peaches, plums and cherries.
Then hardy apples in the fall -
And, God, I loved them all!

I sit now by a reminiscent fire
Content with wine from once-plump summer grapes
And remembrances of
Birds' love songs in my woods
And earthy smells of new life.

Spring will come again
To green the grass and trees
But annuals like me
Will not awaken from
The winter's cold, long sleep.

VIETNAM

Some fought it

Some waited

Some lived it

And all the world wondered

WAR'S PRIORITY

It calls, and should the chance permit,
That I could stay for some slight cause,
I still must go, by honor bound,
Or pride possessed, and weighing not my loss.
I go to kill, or to be killed,
I go to come back home with conscience clear,
I go to do, and say I've done, my part,
I go to cross the valley in between the here and here.
And if I somehow lose the right
To see the fields of home again,
Then count me dead for those alone
Whose love of freedom war's threat can't amend.

THE JOURNEY

Just before I round the crest
Of this last point where I can view
The hills and fields that once were mine alone
In childhood dreams I knew,
Let me look back.

I won't be long, I've promises to keep
Some half a world from here I can't delay.
One backward glance to last
Till someday when again I'll pass this way;

When Spring's sweet breezes
Whisper life to treetops stilled
By winter's chill, some future sun-warmed day,
I'll look down from this hill
On my way home.

VIETNAM CALLS

Though you will stay
And I must go,
So many miles apart,
I'll write each day
I love you so,
And you're first in my heart.
Though life's unfair
And fate a thief,
To steal our fondest dreams.
To know you care
In fond belief
Our lives are one it seems.

And thought the miles may separate
My heart in shackles know
For time and distance only make
My love to live and grow.

LONG DISTANCE

We'll sit awhile and talk about
The things we did today.
Yes, mine was long and lonely, too.
And just like all the rest in its own way.

But now one more has come and gone
And faded in the ranks of past forgotten dates.
This day has seen me doing things
You wouldn't understand, and many fools debate.
I hope that yours was good;
You seem content here with your hand in mine.
Gazing at twilight's first brave stars.
See that bright one on the north's horizon line?!

Then I get up and go inside,
For in reality and sad dismay
That star is just an observation flare,
And you're so many miles away.

THE GREEN FIELDS OF JANUARY

In January's icy grip,
Before the springtime's warming hand
Trips north to spread the living green
Through fields across the land;
When winter's chilling blast seeks cracks
Around the frosted window panes,
I'll only feel the warmth of love
For I'll be home with you again.

I GOT MY NAIL

I got my nail to hang my hat,
Tonight a bed in which to lie,
A space that's mine, and mine alone
To occupy till I go back, or die.

We feel much better now, we're all back safe;
This mattress sure feels good to lie back on and hear
The sounds that made our afternoon complete:
The blackjack cards mixed one on one, "Hey, Joe, another beer?"

I'll watch them make or break their twenty-one
(I'd join the game, but I've a tear to mend)
And talk about the happiness they'll find
Some place that they call home, at rainbow's end.

But now I'll settle for life and breath
To talk to God and Know I'm not alone
And I got my nail to hang my hat
It's not a lot but it's home.
-Viet Nam 1966-

PAPER HERO

Like he died before he hit the ground,
His eyeballs scratched with sand he lay,
When we tallied up our losses
From the enemy guns today.

He was everybody's buddy,
And always poking fun.
A whiz he was on snap shots,
Our outfit's finest gun.

He was everything he should have been
A soldier to a tee,
And when it come to anything,
He was twice as good as me.

So gently like he might could feel
We cart him back to base
And put him in his box to be
His final resting place.

When we sit and shoot the bull tonight
We'll talk about our loss
He's hero of the day all right,
He wins without a toss.

"You think he'll get a medal?"
"Why, I should sure hope so!"
He's number one when plumb stone dead,
But that's the way with heroes.

So he'll be writ a hero
In the hometown news tomorrow;
They'll speak of freedom's part he played
To hide his family's sorrow.

They'll picture him the way they should
With courage that he lacked.
It's not my place to tell them
He got it in the back.

LOOKING BACK

Am I the one whom I recall
Guided by some unseen hand
To destiny half a world away
Here on this distant strand?

It can't be me, his hand is clean.
Unblemished, and that face you see.
Is washed with innocence, now look at mine:
It can't be me.

But sometimes I can share,
In memory, his dreams
Of how he plans to change the world
And what he'll say in walks with kings.

The world is his, and at command
His every wish was but to ask,
And if on any road denied,
Its highest hill is but a trivial task.

He knows not the ties and binds
That life and war caused me to don,
And he's so happy in his way…
Am I to tell him what's beyond?

Am I a puppet on a string
Must my whole life depend on chance?
Am I the one who shaped my way,
Or just a pawn of circumstance?

Written in Viet Nam 1966

OUR DEBT

Another year is over.
Rotation, stateside, and home
A moment of mutual sadness,
Then he turns, and leaves her alone.
And this is the best her life offers
One year, and he's gone home alive.
Many the tear that others have shed
For the many who didn't survive.
And those who must morn the loss
Of the ones who don't come home
May have an ally whose loss is the same
A world away and unknown.
Whatever their payment or reason
They comfort the ones who must fight it
Though <u>theirs</u> has been the terror
God! <u>They</u> must live it or die it.
Many a burden they've lightened;
Many a load they bore:
The faces whose names are forgotten
Our women -- our ladies -- of war.

**CHANGING OF THE GUARD
FROM FATHER TO SON**

PEOPLE....

It has been said that people come into our lives for a reason,
or a season, or for a lifetime.
This section is a tribute to the people who have had
a role in shaping who we are.

POP'S LAST VISIT

When you died
And broke my anchor chain
You did not know
The constant you had given;
The safety of just knowing
You were there.

You came back sometimes;
Ten years ago you sat upon my bed
And told me things would be all right;
To trust myself.
Somehow we knew
Your task was through.

I did OK at length
But I still miss your strength.

OUR TIME

I have been a part
Of many lives;
Some for a fleeting moment,
Some still remain.

And they a part of mine;
I saw the world
Through many eyes,
So it was always new.

I am now composed
Of all the paths and passions
Of all the hopes and dreams and loves
Of those held dear.

Our paths would merge
And often then diverge
Some with a smile
And some with tears.

(continued)

(Our Time Continued)

I hope we truly shared.
But I can only judge
What I received;
I hope I gave as much.

I tried to show to each
Their special gifts.
I made them – for the most part – smile;
I hope that they still do.

I truly tried
To make our time a special time,
To – for a while –
Completely be a part of us.

I tried to glean
The best and special parts of love,
To not sink in the tedium
Of promises unkept.

But the thing I could not give
Was any promise of tomorrow,
Assurance that things would not change,
Or would.

Perhaps these other lives and loves
Have kept me now from being close,
Prevented ties exclusive and unique,
Assured a future loneliness.

Each ended, yes,
But our time did not starve for love
Or long for soon-lost dreams
Or die the normal, lengthy, painful death.

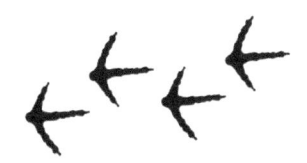

TRIBUTE TO MY SON

It all started
Those years ago
When you made me a father
You grew with uncertain hand
I strived to play the roles
Of teacher, mentor,
Outdoor companion,
A guide through troubled years
Then for a time
I had to let you find your path.
I saw you tall and proud
And off to war

You knew
If freedom's to be earned
Each generation takes it's turn.
Then you became a father
You played all the roles I had
And more – and well
Somewhere along our journey
You became my hero,
My friend my son.

FREE MAN

I've seen the cactus blooming
In the Texas summertime,
Seen Spanish moss a-hanging
In Mississippi's humid clime.

I've milked cows in old Wisconsin,
And lumberjacked in Maine;
I've walked the land from South to North
Following golden grain.

From the Sunshine State to Washington
I've picked anything they grow;
Put all I've seen together,
And there's not much left to show.

If I'm too soiled to thumb a truck,
Then I just hop a freight;
Oh, I'm a hobo sure enough,
But I've seen what makes a country great.

I've chopped wood for three square meals,
Met People bad and nice;
To pay for what I've learned from each
Would take a kingdom's price.

This whole fine land is home to me.
Supplies my tutors, meals and clothing;
I'm sorry I can pay no tax,
But fourteen per cent of nothing's nothing.

My meals are free and varied.
I've got free travel through the land.
With collar soiled, but conscious clean.
Match that job, if you can.

THE GIRL IN LINE

Her name, I can't remember;

She was there just by chance I suppose.

We spoke as friends, as indeed we were

But for time for a friendship to grow.

Trapped by a line, we waited

And while others complained of delay

We came away happy and richer

For one hour along the same pathway.

FREEDOM

Freedom almost died last week
When you almost convinced yourself
That you could live without it.
And someone nearly went away
Someone good
By being someone else
Someone I didn't know.
But you stayed
And freedom's yet unsacrificed
For room and board
I'm glad you did not deal away
Yourself.

JUDY AND ME

Conversation flavored with tea
That's good times for Judy and me.
Laughing thru the good and bad
Rebuilding ourselves and the dreams we had
Sharing our thoughts that others don't see
That's the way with Judy and Me.

She makes things bright on rainy days
She smiles and chases the blues away.
Open and honest that's the key
And that's friendship for Judy and me.

ALLWAYS

Allways.
Our word
For constance
For inclusion
For all I do
Or think
Or am.

It tells
That we're not
Just together,
But rather,
Vital counterparts
Of some inclusive whole.

KEN

He brought all outdoors
To each room he stepped into
The range, the wind, the action
Of the cowboy life he knew.

No job too tough, no day too long
No eight to five for him
It was saddle, spurs and sagebrush
From sunup to twilights dim.

He loved family, friends, and fishing,
Pickups and mountain mornings;
Cowcamps, sunshine and moonlight,
Sixguns and saddle horses.

He rode a trail of silence
Found a way that few have known
He heard his heart, he found his peace
Gave us a pattern, then rode off alone.

DREAMS

How long since you
Have dared to dream?
How long have lonely days
Doing what others think you must
Obscured your dreams?

How many times
Have others dashed your dreams,
Left you to try to find
The shattered pieces?

Give me your dreams
I'll handle them with care;
Let me dream along with you
And watch those dreams come true.

FUEL

I write better

When I'm hungry

For you

Or company

Or even food.

PILOTS

They're off to the skies
And beyond
Seeking their own form
Of self-destruction.
Hurling their toys
Toward each other
Toward the ground
So they can talk
Or be talked about
In bars.

INDOOR PLUMBING

My generation's almost passed
Along with things you cannot grasp.
Things you could not do without
Were not around in our old house.

Now we have the modern things
Like microwaves and phones that ring
All night and day, and go along
Wherever we go and play our songs.

There's 900 channels on TV;
We got along with only three.
TVs were black and white and small,
And now they cover one whole wall.

Things make life better, sure enough,
But I'm sure the nine of us
Would have been glad to trade them all
For a bathroom down the hall.

Cause we would need to take a hike
Even in the darkest night
In winter, summer, spring or fall
Just to answer nature's call.

Sometimes in rain or snow or sleet
Or smelly times in summer's heat;
Your generation thinks that strange,
But that's just how things were back then.

Those times are gone, and sure as heck
We do not miss those midnight treks.
We now have most everything
To make chores and life a simple thing.

But if you didn't have for some few hours
An inside toilet seat and shower,
I'll bet you, too, would trade them all
To have a bathroom down the hall.

TESSA

Beautiful girl
Half-way to womanhood,
With talent, intellect,
And all the tools you need
To be anything you choose.
You have support
And love and guidance
Of those who hold you dear.
But what we want most for you to be
Is happy
And yourself.

LAINE

Barefoot boy with summer's tan
With his whittling knife in hand,
School is out, so now he's free
Playing underneath the trees.

Fruit from the orchard; still too green;
Wading in the pasture stream;
Climbing hills just cause they're there;
Free to roam without a care.

With years to go 'ere grownup fears,
No bills, no clock, no heartache tears,
Gift for Grandma straight from heaven,
We need no more than Laine at seven.

RETREAT

I watched you walk away aloof
Your logic now renewed
Yet for brief moments,
I reached you.

Why did you shy
Each time I made
An obvious trespass
On some painful pathway?

Did I almost reach some secret,
Some unfounded fear,
Some unhealed wound
Left by someone once held dear?

Was love replaced by logic,
Your fantasies by goals?
Your message's dichotomy
Leaves volumes yet untold.

Give me your trust,
Tell me your hopes and fears,
Show me your dreams;
I'll handle them with care.

THE BARRIER

I wanted to say something.
I said nothing at all.
I wanted to tell you
How nice it was to share your evening.
I wanted to tell you
How good you made me feel.
I wanted to tell you
What a special person you are.
I wanted to touch you
But didn't know how.

THE HOMEPLACE FIRE

Only in my memory can I now go
A place and time long gone.
With Mom and Pop long dead
Their ghosts must wander now a barren hill.

Why then this sadness
For what has not been for all these years?
For bodies warmed and meals prepared
On wood fires.

For barely getting by
For bonds solidified
By needing all we all could do
For love, for laughter, toil and tears.

Yes, it changed
But somehow stayed the same
And lives beyond the fire
In memories and all we are.

August 11, 2004

MY MARK

I didn't make my mark upon the world
That I said I would when I was twenty-one
I still don't bask in radiance
Of the glories I have won.
I've fallen short of almost all
The goals that count for score
That guarantee a name in bronze
And open all the doors.
But the world forgets as time goes on
Each person starts anew
And as no one before or since
I made my mark on you.

THE PACE

You are a friend and lover, too
But dearest, something further:
In many subtle ways
You are my better.
This is not a threat to me;
I outgrew that some years ago,
But I find in pacing you
I'm somewhat slow.
You encourage excellence
Not of deeds but of the mind
When you look at me please tolerate
The mediocrity that you may find.
Don't let me hold you back.
Don't hate me later to now spare my pride.
I feel your destiny is greater
I will not let you break your stride.
Be all that you can be,
And when you crest each hill,
Smile when remembering me
And love me still.

APRIL

The harshness of winter is over,
And April has taken her place,
With the grace of a breeze in the willow,
The softness of sun on my face.

Yet I know of the storms that have ravaged
I know of the pain and the tears
Accosted, you stood strong but gentle
Resilient, unyielding to fears.

The trials and heartaches behind you,
Life anew you embrace as a friend
Like the new earth washed by your namesake's showers
That whispers that all will mend.

THE GUIDE

It's dark
So hold my hand
Don't be afraid
I've been this way by day.

I have the eyes
To find dim images and silhouettes
That bound the path ahead
Even in the moonless night.

Scan ahead
Don't look to exact the path
Scant hours hence
We'll see by sunrise glow.

You may then find
You need my hand no more
And you upon a brighter way
May go while caring still.

HELP

It seems when I need help the greatest
Fate sends someone who
Will just accept the way I am
And this time it sent you.

Somewhere through your pain and travels
You seemed to somehow learn the art
To give freely of your friendship
To kindly soothe and mend the hurts.

Thank you for your patient listening
Thank you for the time we shared.
Today the road's not quite as steep
For moments yesterday you cared.

OLD PHOTOGRAPHS

I browsed the tattered greys and browns
Recordings of the way things were
Which now define the way things are,
So when we see those dear ones now
We see the way that they still see themselves.

As if anticipating being seen
We try to be as we would someday seem.
That makes us later laugh,
Because we weren't, and aren't
Yet we still pose.

Do we know we screen the pain
And photograph the things we hold most dear?
The toil, regrets, and pain remain
In unrecorded third dimension
Soft, unfocused memories.

Again to view the things then new
To whet again truth dulled by time
To see the smiles --
The hurts don't show;
The photographs are kind.

THE BATTLE

When the ideal and the real collide
We oft inject the fatal flaw
And so reject the purest choice
Because we want it all.

We wish it so, we want it so
But somehow did not see
We walked away from all the best
For what it cannot be.

Constrained by our convictions
And biased by our sins
Sometimes love is not enough
Sometimes the dragon wins.

NO THANKS

I brought in your things
Made sure you had the things you need
Ran the errand for you up the street
Came back and fixed supper
Pork chops, gravy, rice, and veggies
Ice cream for dessert
Washed the dishes
Cleaned the kitchen.
A thank you would be welcome
But not expected.

PASSION

I see you up on the horse
And know your passion.
Strong, tall and confident
Your bodies meld
Your will controls the whole
Of power, form and grace.

You hurl the challenge at yourself
To do, to be, to push the limits
Not only to achieve, to win
But to seize the fruit of life
And squeezing every drop
Of nectar on your tongue.

I see you up on the horse
I see the fire inside
And know you'll never feel
The fire go out
Nor passion die
Nor lose the lust for life.

CHANCE MEETING

There is no lonely
Like the lonely of an airport
And the plane full of empty faces
Life hidden in the blank looks
Of those who are forced by chance
Upon each other.
Amid gazes seeing nothing
Your smile.
Not bold and broad or forced.
Just revealing that you – perhaps
Dare to care.
We talked – at first of nothing-
Of people, places, happenings
Then of ideas, ideals.
We even dared to share
A little of ourselves
How short a time.
How rare how savored
That makes hours only moments
But moments that can last always
I cherish them as time not spent
But rather lived.
Why then this sadness?
That makes me look for you in every empty crowd;
Your Smile.

FLIGHT

Lifted by the magic of
The mind of man
To look upon the world
As our fathers only dreamed of.

THE ONES THAT GOT AWAY

We set the hook,
And the game begins;
Sometimes the fish
We never see wins.

We'll never know
How big it was;
The biggest one ever
We fanaticize.

For the ones we caught
The challenge was done
And oft not remembered
Whenever we won.

But the sweetness of almost
The thrill of the chase,
Unlike the victories,
Can't be erased.

And so it's been
With a lady or two
I went home without
When the night was through.

We remember each one
That wanted to play
But for some twist
Chose to pass that day.

One got cold feet
In the hotel room,
One's mom nearly caught us,
One's husband came home.

I've seen the looks
That thrilled to the bone
And would have meant "yes"
But for time alone.

So a toast to the ones
Who couldn't stay;
We came so close,
But they got away.

EVERYBODY DIES

Everybody dies.
The most noble way
Is on disputed hills
For freedom's cause.
But I came back
With only unseen scars.
Some go
With protracted pain;
Some in a place
Where care is just a job.
Some slip away
As in a quiet sunset.
How ever I go
I hope it is while I am
Loved and admired
By those I love.
Everybody dies.
I just want mine to be
Not a relief
But a surprise.

OUTDOORS.....

*"This old house isn't much to look at,
      but I don't live inside very much."*

George L. Haas (my father) September 1979

WORLDS

Let me show you my mountains
Sleep with me in the meadow
Among wildflowers in the afternoon
Bathe with me in the stream
Watch the stars seem closer
See through my eyes.

Then show me your world
Through your eyes
And how to touch it
With your fingers
A gentler touch
Let me be you.

TIME LAUGHS

When we obscure

Behind closed doors

The sunset's glow

Time laughs

That we should spend our hours so.

THE FEATHER

When Michael came to New Mexico –
It was '91 I recall –
He came for the hunt of a lifetime
For elk on Valle Vidal.

Our spirits were high as the mountain
Though we knew the odds were low
When he came for his bull of a lifetime
He was only bringing a bow.

A hunt with a bow is the hard way to go;
Six times he had journeyed west,
For a trophy that proved so elusive,
Had been a ten-year quest.

Six miles we labored with heavy packs,
Till we came to a favorite place
Beside a stream in Foreman Canyon
That we'd call home for nine days.

Now heat is a curse hunting high country elk
And each day was hot and dry.
But there aren't second chances on Valle Vidal,
So we gave it our very best try.

The elk holed up in the deepest draws
Where the currents blew every which way,
And the dry twigs snapped with the softest step;
The mountain was making us pay.

We were out six days with nothing to show
But blisters and sweaty clothes
That we washed along with ourselves in the creek,
Cause an elk has a very keen nose.

The sixth afternoon on a ridge near camp –
We had not seen an elk all day –
A pair of grouse walked out in the trail
Where it appeared they intended to stay.

"I'm not going home empty handed."
Mike said as he nocked a shaft,
And the arrow flew and his aim was true,
And we took fresh meat back to camp.

I plucked a feather from the grouse's tail;
I kept it and didn't know why,
Till I was alone and the hunt was done
And I had an idea to try.

The seventh day broke red in the east
We felt a change in the air,
And the sign was heavy on Foreman ridge;
The elk had just been there.

"They'll be back at dusk." I whispered,
And I hoped that it was true.
So we backed off a ways and we spent the day
Planning and trying to snooze.

Late that day back at the clearing
We watched as the sun dipped low,
Then there was an elk, then two, then more,
And we knew they would pass below!

Behind the cows came the canyon boss
He didn't see anything strange
As he answered the challenge we bugled;
He stepped into the bow's deadly range.

Was it my heart or Mike's I heard pounding
As he pulled his bow to full draw?
The arrow flew and we both knew
That the canyon boss was ours.

Time never passes so slowly
As when the arrow is freed.
It seems to hang in a graceful arc
Though it flies nearly too fast to see.

But the bull took one step too many
And the shaft struck a little far back
We saw him stagger as it sliced through his liver;
He left plenty of blood to track.

The meadow that moments before was full
Of elk was now empty and still,
And the last we saw they crossed the draw
To the woods on the opposite hill.

In the fading light we hit his trail
We didn't have much of a lamp.
The blood flow slowed and the sun sank low,
And we had to go back to camp.

We ate a supper we didn't taste
And we didn't talk much that night.
We sacked out early but didn't sleep,
And we were up before first light.

We found the trail from the night before,
But the tracking was dreadfully slow.
With no blood trail it was step by step,
And our spirits were getting low.

To a hunter it's more than a trophy
Or a story that can't be told,
For an animal not recovered
Will eat at your very soul.

Tomorrow the hunt would be over;
Tomorrow Mike left for home
But he had no taste for more of the hunt,
He wanted <u>this</u> bull for his own.

We crisscrossed and tracked on our hands and knees
And tried every trick we knew,
But the odds that were low were getting worse,
And we both knew it was true.

Three hours we covered each inch of the hill
Each movement with diligent patience,
And what we saw at the crown of the hill
Caused despair to give way to elation.

114

The elk of a lifetime lay dead on the trail
The arrow clean up to the fletch;
And we both wept and we didn't know why,
Relief, remorse, joy, or which?

The seventh day of the seventh hunt,
And maybe it wasn't a sign,
But one of the beams on the big bull's rack
Showed seven magnificent tines.

And was it just a coincidence
As we sweated under our loads
That the place on the hill that the big elk fell
Was seven miles from the road?

A grouse feather hangs on a plaque on Mike's wall,
And few know the story but me.
It hangs by the bull of a lifetime;
The consolation that wasn't to be.

JUST ONE LAST CAST

Its awfully late;
I guess I should be leaving right away
But there is just no better place
To end a day.
It's like a different world;
It just seems timeless here
So peaceful, so serene
With no war or hate or fear
Just God and fish and me
And I've had better days
At least I've caught more fish
But that's no way to rate today
It hasn't been an easy day
To break that fly rod tip just made me sick;
I must admit that sandwich wasn't much
After soaking in the creek.
I've got a grand finale
Waiting at the river bend
Where ol' grandad trout took line and lure and all,
And made me out a fool last weekend.
I told her I'd be home by six
But I'm sure I couldn't feed her that old line
With that flashlight peeking from my pocket.
Oh well, I should be home by nine.
With supper cold she'll pace the floor
And say that I don't love her, I've a notion,
But could she if she only knew
That here I love this whole creation.

THE HUNT

I hunted the elk and I got it!
Came out with a big one last Fall
But for all the thrill of the hunt and the chase,
It's not just the elk I recall.

Spent a week in the sun-drenched Rockies.
I watched the aspens turn gold.
Saw the world as it readied for winter
Watched the world's greatest drama unfold.

Packed all my needs in a rucksack,
Not a care or a trouble went in.
To take in a part of the daily mundane
Would be a terrible sin.

Strained my lungs and my muscles and sinew
From first light til way after dark.
If not for the love of the mountain,
No paycheck could buy all that work.

Have you spent the night in a spike camp?
Been alone with your thoughts in the wild?
Made a friend of all that wildness?
Put aside the façade for a while?

I'm back at my job in the city,
The real world by some accounts.
The time I spend here just reminds me
Of the things that, for me, really count.

When the sun again rises South of East,
And the blue skies of Autumn begin;
When the first frost touches the canyons,
I'll be back to my mountain again!

(continued)

(The Hunt cont'd)

Back to the honest and real world,
Back to the creek's gurgling mirth,
Back to the meadows and forests of home,
Back to my real peace on earth.

OUR CABIN IN THE HILLS

I've a cabin in the hills,
A place to cure the daily ills,
Where neighbors all wear fur or feathers,
And family and friends can gather.

Where kids and dogs can safely roam
In the forest we call home,
Or romping in the pasture fields
At the cabin in the hills.

Far away from city strife
To share with friends and kids and wife
On the porch in evening's still,
I've a cabin in the hills.

MY PLACE

One morning when the dawn erupts with violent still
There comes, a faint enticing voice from the hill,
And those beyond, unknown to most,
Unheard by all, save those who lust
To blindly do its bid, and guessed by most unreal.

For those who find their place can't understand
Some's happiness to be untied, unrooted to the land.
Their life must be as tangible and real
As ours, undone, unchained but for the seal
Which bonds us to the restless wind and shifting sand.

Some hear her from the highest hill, some from the enchantment's sea.
Respecting neither time nor place, she holds us jealously.
Unsure am I of how or why, or even of whence from.
But ever-knowing of the certainly that she will come
And, in her chosen time, pick me

You may wake to find me gone,
Or see my feet yearn restlessly to roam:
Again I must, to wanderlust, a tribute pay.
Then please don't bid me stay;
My place moves on!

ALASKA SUMMER

I hunted the fish, and I caught 'em
Enough to last till next season,
But for all the love of the chase and the fight,
I came for a much different reason.

Filled with awe, watched Denali at sunrise,
Felt how big and how wild and how empty,
Saw the bustle of the boats in the harbor,
Making most of the season of plenty.

Saw the rivers swell with the snow melt;
Watched the glaciers rumble and fall;
Saw the caribou, bear, and moose with their young;
I was there! I was part of it all!

There's a place in the North like no other
Unforgiving, with hardship and pain,
But a place of bounty and beauty
That calls me again and again.

MAN VS NATURE

It snows, in white serene and peace,
But man can't bear perfection by some unseen hand.
He rushes out to scar and mar;
To violate this newfound virgin land.

In vain repeat the tide
Comes lapping twice a day.
Consuming change that reeks of man's vile touch,
And tries to drive the fools away.

The wind, thought it blows night and day
And shifts the sands to meet
God's perfect plan, it can't erase
The scars of endless regularity of restless feet.

And then when all the elements have tried
To hide the arch-mistake of man's just being here,
The darkness comes to hide us with a truth denying camouflage
Till morning breaks to rule again sincere.

MENDING THE BREAK

To Renee, with love....
Sometimes we have the opportunity
to put an important relationship back together.

FIRST STEPS

Where will these halting first steps lead,
Me back to you; you back to me?
Will our paths again diverge,
Or love allow our lives to merge?

We stumbled once in our pursuit
For life together 'neath one roof,
And while our needs were both the same
We tried too hard and all in vain.

So we begin a different quest
To focus on the very best
That our relationship can be:
Friends forever, you and me.

And where our love will choose to go
We won't direct and cannot know.

OUT OF TOUCH

What are you feeling now?
There was a time
Short days ago
I felt it, too, and knew.

Now I grope in the dark
Will this end as it began?
Don't linger now
To merely save my pride.

TIME IS KIND

Time is kind
It brought me back to you
With places only stops along the way
And all the hills I climbed
Were just to look for you
Except I didn't know it then.
I learned from many people
Some a lot like you
Some very different: they didn't seem a threat
I ran
And did a hundred things
To chase your dream away.
But all was not a waste
I've memories to share with you
And years to share them
While we make tomorrow's memories
I've learned I want you there in every one.
Because I learned more:
That only time with you is life
The time between was just the avenues
That brought me back to you.

APRIL 301TH

I tore off April's page today
And looked at all my daily notes.
I remember 30 days ago:
Excitement
Anticipation
Love and optimism.
How could so much change;
Could I have made it not change?
Springtime's first warm month
Was so cruel to my dreams,
The tearing of the page
Ripped pieces from my heart.

THE FIREMAKERS

We kindled the fire
And it blazed high.
But any new flame
Is subject to the wind and rain.
It warmed us both
Those years ago
Things were different then
So were we.
The flame flickered, then went out
Smothered by our parting
People, places things
And even we didn't know
How well we banked the embers
So well they glowed for years
And burned a mark.
Then like winter morning coals
Blown gently to revive the glow
With trembling hands we added fuel
Watched the growing warmth
And smiled
Knowing the house would soon be warm.

FULFILLED

The dreams I dream at night
Are my dreams come true by day;
All the hopes of all the years
I now live as each day's thrills;
The sunshine of my life today
Is the warmth by me tonight;
The love of my entire life
Is the lady in my life;
This loving woman in my world
Is the reason for my world.

MY LOVE GROWS NEAR

My love grows near.
We've lonely days apart,
Now only hours separate
My missing half of heart.

I am my own;
I've done quite well alone.
That was before
My soul found its true home.

Now when hours parted stretch to days,
I feel some vital part of me
Is somewhat wandering lost
And waiting once again to be.

But heart, be of great cheer,
Our love grows near.

THE WISH

If I could make one wish
And change one thing
I don't know what
That wish would be.

Every single thing gone wrong
So intertwined
With things so fondly
Now held close.

If I could wish
That we could start all over
Would caution kill
The thrills we had?

If I could wish
For some healing compromise
Would one of us - or both -
Lose something of ourselves?

If I could wish
You'd take me back
Someday would the ending
Be the same?

If I could wish
For all the hurt to stop
Would that mean
Love too would end?

Whatever I could change
With any granted wish
Would entail a risk
I dare not take.

FOR ALL THE WRONG REASONS

I tried to tell myself
It could not work.
There are so many fatal flaws.

I tried to disbelieve
Lacking evidence that this could be
With no examples otherwise.

I tried to justify
I had to minimize the hurts
And love cannot be quantified.

I tried to go
Almost convinced I could
Ignore the emptiness
Forget the warmth which flowed
To fill the cold dark corners.

MY DAUGHTER....

Being a father to my daughter as she grew
was the most rewarding, enlightening and joyous job I ever had.

JENNIFER AT EIGHT

Reading books or riding bikes

Or skating through the neighborhood;

A wonder halfway in between

A babe and mystic womanhood.

So she goes expanding her world

Spreading wings that soon will lift her

From the nest that I built for her

Breaking bonds that now protect her.

Personified enthusiasm

Unaware of widening chasms

Leaning less on our relation

That must grow toward separation.

She comes back far enough to see

Around the bend to look for me.

Today she's mine and likes it that way

She'll be her own some too soon someday.

JENNIFER AT TWELVE

Four years of change
Since I described
Your simple world
Of eight years old.

Four years more mature
Four years of pride for me
To see you building values
To see you choosing well.

Four years of firsts:
Boyfriend. Heartbreak.
Toe shoes. High heels.
And other introductions to a woman's world.

Four years of changing tastes:
For gold. Earrings.
Judy Blume.
Some boys aren't so bad.

Four years of goodbyes:
To grammar school. Braces.
PJs with feet.
A world I could protect you from.

Four years hence
You will have begun
To chart a course to guide your way
For years to come.

Four years more
Who will you be?
I only guess
At your more complex world
But you'll be somewhat less
My little girl.

JENNIFER AT SIXTEEN

Years ago
As you took your first halting steps
I kept you just beyond
My finger tips
Just in case.

I held onto the bike seat
When you seemed ready
I let you slip beyond my reach
I ran beside, then stopped and watched
With pride and apprehension.

I stood by the window
As you first drove away
Into a world
So unforgiving
You did fine - I knew you would.

I saw the young man
Hold the door
As you climbed inside
I hoped he knew
How important you are to me.

It's not mistrust
That makes the turning loose so hard
It's because you are each time
A little further out of reach
But I still reach for you
Just in case.

JENNIFER AT TWENTY

Each time we talk long distance
I recall the way I chided you
For tying up the phone
Four years ago.

Four years and worlds away.
Were things more simple then?
Better? Worse?
Or only different?

Since then, we have taken both our worlds
Put them in jars
And shook them
Till nearly everything has changed.

I took apart the world you knew
You took my little girl away
Yet through motherhood, the moves, the marriages
Our love endured.

Do you know how proud I am of you
As you go out to slay your dragons?
Do you know how good it feels
To have you as my hero?

I am concerned
For all the roles
That you must play
Student, mother, worker, wife and friend.

And a little sad because you have
So little time to be just you
And because we have
So little time together.

I hope that someday we will have
Lives that aren't so far apart,
For now I'll cherish all the calls
And think of you a hundred times between.

Try not to be concerned with change
For as much as anything
I do believe in these:
Our love, and you.

JENNIFER AT TWENTY-FOUR

What to decide and what to choose
So much at stake, so much to lose
Even when you know the score
Like Jennifer at twenty-four.

We all must choose before we see
What will be with clarity
Then we fight our private war
Like Jennifer at twenty-four.

Too soon you shed your youthful bliss
Succumbing to a Judas kiss
A promise that is heard no more
By Jennifer at twenty-four.

A mother's love used as a tool
To bind you to the altered rules
And now exposed, you can't ignore
Not Jennifer at twenty-four.

Emerging from illusion's haze
Recovering from the darkest days
With focus on what lies before
For Jennifer at twenty-four.

You'll triumph as I know you can
You have before, you will again
To live the happy days in store
For Jennifer at twenty-four.

LOVE WAITS

Sometimes fate separates us from
the ones we hold most dear.
If we endure, the wait will form even stronger bonds.

THE WAIT

I waited once before
Not knowing what would be.
But then we talked,
Loved, lived and planned.

Then I could see
Love reflected in your eyes
And knew somehow
You'd be – we'd be – OK.

Now I wait alone
The caring friends unable
To know you'll be – we'll be – again,
Unable to replace the you in us.

I wait in silent vigil
With machines I sometimes hate,
And when I talk
I wonder if you hear.

Never has there been
Two weeks we didn't talk.
While you sleep I hope you know
I'm here; I'll wait.

BACK FROM THE BRINK

You smiled today.
You seemed to know
How far you'd come,
Back from the brink.

An awful journey
We both made alone
While you slept
While I wept.

In time you'll heal
We've still a journey left
But together now.
You smiled today.

BEHIND THE NEED

Are there needs that you no longer have,
Or changed so that I don't recognize
The feelings that once lead to love, Do I no longer satisfy?

Once we laughed and talked and played
Awakened an imperative sublime
With Passions peaked made love;
Exhausted, fell asleep intertwined

But now we only love
When driven by a pent up need
We curb the lust and turn away
Turn on the set or read.

I miss the joys that spawned the lust
I miss time when my touch thrilled
I miss being something more
Than just a need fullfilled.

FOR LOVE AND DUTY'S SAKE

Before a trace of eastern glow,
I rise before the clock implores -
It only woke me once in March -
And do my regimented chores.

I call at six
From just outside your hall;
They know me now;
They make exceptions when I call.

I relate to you the day just past,
And just in case you hear,
While I recite a dialog or read
I try to hide my fear.

Two, three, four times a day
I step from world to world.
Reality is vague, tomorrow but a concept
As I contain this inner turmoil.

I feel so weak
For even having thoughts of me;
I'm not the one at risk,
I'm well, awake and free.

I'm sometimes home when darkness comes.
Can I get through one more?
The wine I pour is not to celebrate
It dulls the sting and soothes the aching sore.

I see you every day,
Yet I've never felt so much alone
Or missed you more
While life goes on, and on.

FURRY FRIENDS

Our animals become not just pets, but our friends,
our comfort and our families.
They are gone too soon,
but in our memories always.

DAISY AND ME

Up at the cabin
And running free
That's living life
For Daisy and me.

By the creek
Sitting under a tree
God gave today
To Daisy and me;

No need to talk
Her head on my knee
That's conversation
For Daisy and me.

Sharing a pillow
And off to sleep,
Sweet end of the day
For Daisy and me.

Our time together
Too short may be,
But it's unquestioned love
For Daisy and me

BOOMER

We found you at the so-called shelter
You doomed to die not knowing love,
Never with a chance to be
All that you could give and share.

You knew only past neglect,
Abused by some unfeeling hand;
Discarded for your body's flaws
Despite your loving, gentle soul.

But we saw in you something more
If we but mend your painful past-
That you'd give back without reserve
And become a part of us.

You came to us with hopeful trust,
Knowing somehow that you must
Rely on someone –
You chose us.

GREY CAT

You came to the farm without a name or pedigree
But all the tools you needed to survive
Your independence, cunning, stealth and will:
I saw this in you piercing, yellow-green eyes.

Where did you start your life
Needing no one, trusting no one?
I like to think
The choice was your own.

When our two worlds first crossed
You'd melt away each time the front door creaked.
I glimpsed you through the bushes
Me wondering about you; you mistrusting me.

Then you dared to let me closer
As I went about my outdoor chores
And ever under your intense green stare
We seemed to share a common bond.

We shared this friendship for a year
Each day more accepting of each other's trespass.
Did you see in me no threat
And just a predator like you?

When I found you by the road today
I touched you for the first time
As I took your lifeless body
To the place we honor passed-on pets.

But you were your own, and never owned
You lived on your own terms.
I'll miss the uncertain bond and truce we had
And your unblinking, yellow-green gaze.

A DEATH IN THE FAMILY

I look through the cold glass door
At the empty patio;
We washed the door on Saturday
And made the nose prints go away.
In a sleepy daze again
This morning I went to let you in.
And when it snowed three days ago
I looked for dog tracks in the snow.
Thirteen summers went so fast
All too soon your time here passed.
We grew with you; you grew with us,
Asking nothing but our love.
The house is not the same tonight
Without you snoring by the fire.
How long until I do not stare
Through the door to see you there.

About the Author
Or
How I Got to Be This Way

I was born in Caldwell County NC in 1944, the last of nine children. My father was a carpenter and a farmer, as was I, until I was nineteen. My mother was a homemaker and everything she had to be, because we would have been below the poverty line if we had had one back then. Her mother had been a school teacher and a poet, and so my mother instilled in me the love of literature at an early age. I began writing poetry when I was twelve.

After high school, I enlisted in the Air Force. After 8 years I had my MS in Electrical Engineering and a commission. Among other things, I have been a carpenter, farmer, electrical technician, engineer, flight test engineer, weapons developer, hunting guide, interior decorator, and writer.

Spending time outdoors has always been the passion of my life. When I was growing up hunting and fishing was not just for recreation, but it helped feed the family. I still enjoy those pursuits, as well as camping, hiking and enjoying time outdoors with our grandchildren. I have been a hunting guide for 36 years, which has been a great satisfaction and has provided the source for many great friendships. Of note is my friend, Faye Henry that I met at a hunting camp over 30 years ago. Without her assistance, encouragement, and expertise in publishing, Lives In Poetry would never have happened. Look closely and you will find her among the pages.

I currently live in Las Cruces NM with my wife Renee. Between the two of us we have 4 children and 8 grandchildren. I previously wrote outdoor articles for The Albuquerque Journal, but this website is my first publishing experience. I hope you enjoy the poetry I have written over the years but never published. That book is in work and will be available soon.

I also have other books and articles that will be available after publication of Life Ain't a Dress Rehearsal. You will find them on my website at www.LivesInPoetry.com

Cecil D Haas

Thank you for your interest in my poetry.

Published by
Indy Pub

Layout and design by Faye Henry
www.TsVibrations.com

Photos by
Cecil Haas
Faye Henry
Renee Peterson

Contact Information for Cecil is available on his website

www.LivesInPoetry.com

More stories, poems, and a blog are available there for your enjoyment.

Milton Keynes UK
Ingram Content Group UK Ltd.
UKHW051837040823
426344UK00003B/78